NEW TECHNOLOGY

forensic technology

Ian Graham

A⁺
Smart Apple Media

Published in the United States by Smart Apple Media, PO Box 3263, Mankato, Minnesota, 56002

Printed by New Era Printing Co. Ltd, China

Library of Congress Cataloging-in-Publication Data

Graham, Ian, 1953-
  Forensic technology / Ian Graham.
     p. cm. -- (New technology)
  Includes index.
  Summary: "Describes the technology used by forensic scientists to gather and analyze evidence from crime scenes"--Provided by publisher.
  ISBN 978-1-59920-532-8 (library binding)
  1. Forensic sciences--Juvenile literature. 2. Forensic sciences--Technological innovations--Juvenile literature. 3. Criminal investigation--Juvenile literature. I. Title.
  HV8073.8.G734 2012
  363.25--dc22
                                    2010044238

June 2011
CAG 1652

9 8 7 6 5 4 3 2 1

Credits
Series Editor: Paul Humphrey
Editor: Kathryn Walker
Designer: sprout.uk.com
Illustrations: Stefan Chabluk
Production: Jenny Mulvanny
Picture researcher: Kathryn Walker

Acknowledgements
Cover and title page Greg Pease/Taxi/Getty Images; p.6 Sean Gallup/Getty Images; p.7 Peter Menzel/Science Photo Library; p.8 Brandon Alms/istockphoto.com; p.11 Patrick Landmann/Science Photo Library; p.12 Jim Varney/Science Photo Library; p.13 Dr Gary Settles/Science Photo Library; p.14 istockphoto.com; p.15 Elena Korenbaum/istockphoto.com; p.16 David Parker/Science Photo Library; p.17 Paul Fleet/Shutterstock; p.18 AP; p.19 Joe Mercier/Shutterstock; p.20 Dean Purcell/Getty Images; p.22 Reuters/?Corbis; p.24 used with permission from www.forensicsmicroscopes.com; p.26 Andrew Syred/Science Photo Library; p.27 Jim Craigmyle/Corbis; p.28 istockphoto.com; p.29 (top) Geoff Tompkinson/Science Photo Library; p.29 (bottom) courtesy of EPSRC; p.30 Sebastian Pfuetze/Corbis; p.31 Konstantin Sutyagin/?Shutterstock; p.32 Louise Murray/?Science Photo Library; p.33 Digital Art/Corbis; p.34 Foster & Freeman Ltd.; p.35 courtesy of the US Dept. of Energy's Ames Laboratory; p.36 Antonov Roman/Shutterstock; p.37 James King-Holmes/Science Photo Library; p.38 Wikimedia Commons (Vassil); p.39 Mark Joseph/Getty Images; p.40 Tischenko Irina/Shutterstock; p.41 Larry W. Smith/?Getty Images; p.42 istockphoto.com; p.43 James Steidl/Shutterstock.

This book was prepared for Evans Brothers by Discovery Books Ltd. (www.discoverybooks.net)

contents

introduction 6

CHAPTER 1   **print** evidence   8

CHAPTER 2   **dna** profiling   14

CHAPTER 3   **fire** and explosion   20

CHAPTER 4   **trace** evidence   24

CHAPTER 5   **investigating** death   30

CHAPTER 6   **fakes** and forgeries   34

CHAPTER 7   **cyber** forensics   40

conclusion 42

glossary 44

more information 45

index 46

introduction

Forensic science is the use of science in investigating crimes, and forensic scientists use a great variety of technological tools to analyze evidence in criminal cases—from standard scientific instruments, including microscopes, to custom-built machines using lasers and X-rays.

Looking for evidence Criminals leave strands of hair, fibers from clothing, fingerprints, and other evidence at a crime scene. They always leave something behind, no matter how hard they try not to. They also can't avoid taking something away from the crime scene when they leave. They might carry away mud on their shoes, fragments of glass or carpet fibers on their clothes, or a victim's blood on their hands. These are the pieces of evidence linking a criminal to a crime scene that forensic scientists search for.

Forensic technology Forensic scientists use the latest science and technology to collect and analyze every scrap of evidence that might help to identify a criminal. Evidence collected at a crime scene is sealed in

At a crime scene, investigators collect every bit of evidence they can find. Yellow markers indicate the positions of material that might be evidence.

CRIME LAB

The world's first police crime lab was set up in Lyon, France, in 1910 by Edmond Locard. He was a professor of forensic medicine at the University of Lyon. The crime lab was housed in just two rooms of the town's courthouse. Locard was the first person to say that a criminal always leaves something at a crime scene and takes something away. This idea is now known as Locard's Exchange Principle.

Forensic scientists work in a secure lab equipped with instruments that they use to analyze evidence from crimes.

bags that are not opened again until they are inside a secure crime lab. There, scientists examine the evidence using various instruments and equipment. Forensic scientists extract the maximum amount of information that might lead police officers to the criminal's door and provide the proof needed for a conviction in court. New developments in technology may soon make it possible for some advanced tests to be done at the crime scene, helping police catch criminals more quickly.

Dramatic effect TV shows about forensic scientists and crime scene investigators are very popular, but they can be misleading. For dramatic effect and to fit a complicated investigation into an hour-long time slot, the scientists and their all-powerful technology produce instant results that never fail to solve the crime. In the real world, scientific tests take longer, and the results can be less clear-cut. However, forensic technology and techniques are improving all the time. New ways to use computers, microscopes, lasers, chemical analyzers, and other technology are constantly being developed so that forensic scientists stay one step ahead of criminals.

CHAPTER 1
print evidence

All of us leave fingerprints behind when we touch something, and everyone's fingerprints are different. Even identical twins have different fingerprints. Fingerprints provide one way to identify a particular person and prove that he or she was present at the scene of a crime.

Finding prints Fingerprints are often invisible to the naked eye. These invisible prints are called latent prints. Crime scene investigators lightly brush fine aluminum powder over surfaces where fingerprints are likely to have

A forensic scientist dusts for fingerprints at a crime scene. The dusting powder shows fingerprints on and around the door handle.

been left. The powder sticks to fingerprints and makes them easier to see. Making a latent fingerprint visible is called "developing" the print. Tape is pressed onto a dusted print and then peeled off, lifting the print. The tape, with the print stuck to it, is then stuck down onto a card and taken away for analysis.

Prints on some materials can't be dusted. Absorbent materials, such as paper, soak up the oily liquid in the print and leave nothing for dusting powder to stick to. These materials are treated with chemicals that react with a fingerprint and change color to make it visible. A chemical called ninhydrin is used on paper. It turns purple when it reacts with a fingerprint. Prints on plastic and metal can be revealed by a process called fuming. An object thought to have fingerprints on it is placed in a cabinet with a small pan of superglue. The superglue is heated and the vapor it gives off sticks to the fingerprints, making them visible.

HOW IT WORKS

Human fingertips are covered with raised lines called friction ridges. Their job is to help us grip things. They vary in length and width, forming a unique pattern. Oily sweat constantly comes out of pores (tiny holes in the skin) on top of the friction ridges. It coats the ridges and leaves an oily copy of the pattern of the friction ridges behind when a fingertip touches something. This is a fingerprint.

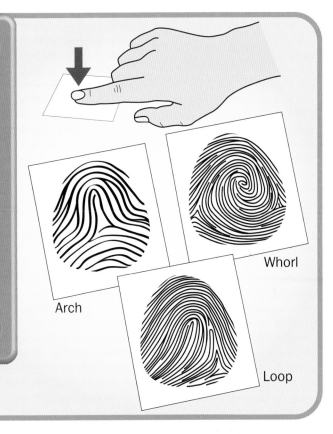

Whorl

Arch

Loop

The lines in all human fingerprints form one of three patterns, called arch, loop, or whorl.

X-rays Researchers from the University of California working at the Los Alamos National Laboratory have found a way to see fingerprints without using powder or chemicals. They discovered they could make fingerprints glow by firing X-rays at them. The oily sweat that forms fingerprints contains a variety of chemicals that come from inside the body. The X-rays make sodium, potassium, and chlorine in the fingerprints glow brightly. This reveals every detail of the prints without destroying or altering them in any way. The technique is called micro-X-ray fluorescence, or MXRF.

WHAT'S NEXT?

Advances in forensic science and technology make it easier for crime investigators to detect evidence, collect it, and analyze it. Wireless technology enables them to send and receive information more easily, wherever they are. In the future, forensic scientists may be able to scan a crime scene with a machine that detects all the fingerprints present and then send them wirelessly for identification.

Multiple prints If two or more people leave fingerprints on top of each other, the usual dusting and chemical methods can't separate them. Now, scientists at Purdue University in Indiana have found a way to separate the prints. Each print contains a unique mixture of chemicals. The scientists have developed a technique called DESI-MS (desorption electrospray ionization mass spectometry) to tell the difference between them and reveal each print separately. Computer software linked to a machine called a mass spectrometer shows the different chemicals present in different colors. The result is a map of the fingerprints, with each person's prints appearing in a different color.

DESI-MS works by spraying electrically charged droplets at the fingerprints.

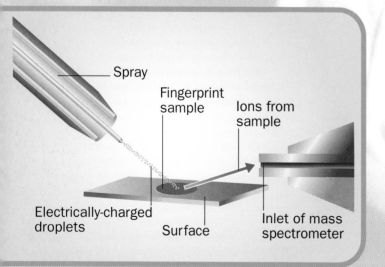

In DESI-MS, a fine electrically charged spray is directed at a surface carrying multiple fingerprints.

A mass spectrometer uses magnetism to identify unknown substances.

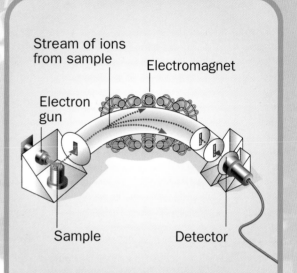

HOW IT WORKS

In a mass spectrometer, charged particles called ions from an unknown substance fly through a tube inside an electromagnet. Air would stop the ions, so the air is sucked out. Magnetic forces make the ions fly in a curve. The shape of the curve depends on the mass of the ions and the strength of the magnet. As the strength of the magnet is turned up, heavier and heavier ions fly all the way through the tube and hit a detector at the end. The strength of the magnet when each type of particle arrives shows the particle's mass and identifies it.

It fires the droplets at just one spot of the sample at a time. The droplets give the atoms and molecules in that section of the fingerprints an electric charge. These charged particles are called ions. Some of the ions evaporate from the surface and are sucked into a mass spectrometer, which identifies them. Then the spray moves on to the next spot on the prints, and so on, until the entire area has been analyzed.

Scanners Fingerprints can be taken from people by using a fingerprint scanner. A finger is pressed against a glass screen, which is scanned to download the print into a computer. The print can then be sent anywhere in the world over the Internet for identification. Many places use fingerprint scanners for added security. Travelers' fingerprints are now scanned at all international airports and seaports in the U.S.

Identifying prints Fingerprints used to be identified by hand. Fingerprint officers had to check thousands of fingerprint record cards, looking for a match with an unknown print. One search could take weeks. Now, unknown prints can be checked against millions of stored prints in a few minutes using a computerized system called AFIS (Automated Fingerprint Identification System).

IAFIS

The FBI (Federal Bureau of Investigation) has the world's biggest AFIS. It is called the Integrated Automated Fingerprint Identification System (IAFIS) because it holds criminal history information as well as fingerprints. The IAFIS holds prints from more than 55 million people that can be searched by computer. Law enforcement agencies can use it 24 hours a day, 365 days a year. They usually receive a response within two hours.

A fingerprint officer tries to identify an unknown print using an Automated Fingerprint Identification System (AFIS).

FOR AND AGAINST

Should the whole population be fingerprinted and the prints stored on an AFIS?

For
- Fingerprinting everyone would make it easier to identify fingerprints left at crime scenes.
- Crimes could be solved faster, saving police time and public expense.

Against
- Many innocent people would object to having their fingerprints taken and stored because of the invasion of their privacy or the feeling that they were being treated like criminals.
- Setting up and running a large database containing millions of fingerprints is very costly.

Making a cast of a shoeprint preserves the print and lets an investigator take it back to the lab for analysis.

The sheet is stuck down on top of the print. The dust and dirt that forms the print sticks to the sheet, which is peeled off, taking the shoeprint with it.

Shoeprints Footprints found at a crime scene can help to identify a suspect. Investigators preserve footprints in soft ground by making a cast of each print using plaster or a material called dental stone. The cast shows all the little nicks and cuts that make each shoeprint unique. Tire tracks are recorded in the same way. A shoeprint on a hard floor can be lifted by using a sticky plastic sheet.

Bullet prints When a bullet is fired, the inside of the gun barrel makes marks on the soft lead bullet. The marks are unique to each gun. By looking at the marks on a bullet under a microscope, forensic scientists can tell which gun fired the bullet. It is harder to prove who fired the gun, especially if fingerprints have been wiped off. Criminals often remember to wipe a gun, but not the empty cartridge cases left behind after a gun has been fired. Until recently, they didn't clean the

HOW IT WORKS

Grooves called rifling spiral down the length of a gun barrel. When a soft lead bullet is fired down the barrel, the rifling grips it and makes it spin. Spinning bullets are more accurate. The rifling marks every bullet a gun fires. No two guns have identical rifling. As a result, bullets can be matched to the gun that fired them by looking at the rifling marks.

By studying marks on a bullet, forensic scientists can tell which gun fired it. Fingerprints on a gun or cartridge case may also help them find out who fired the gun.

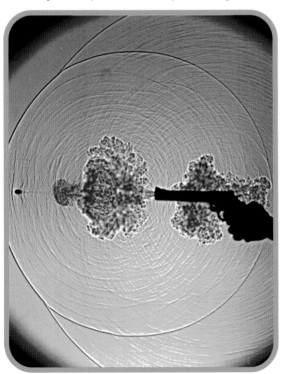

cartridge cases, because everyone thought that the heat produced by firing a gun destroyed fingerprints on them. Then in 2008, scientists at Leicester University in England discovered a way to retrieve fingerprints on cartridge cases.

A fingerprint causes a tiny amount of corrosion (a chemical change) on the bullet's metal case. This is normally invisible. However, if an electric charge is applied to a cartridge case that has been coated with fine black powder, microscopic pits in the metal surface caused by the corrosion attract the powder and the print appears. Cold, or unsolved, cases going back decades could be reopened and perhaps solved using this new technique.

WHAT'S NEXT?

In the future, it may be possible to discover someone's race, sex, and even what they eat from a single fingerprint. Scientists at Imperial College in London, England, have already demonstrated how to do this by analyzing the chemicals dissolved in fingerprints. If further research proves successful, forensic scientists may one day be able to use the same technique to analyze fingerprints from crime scenes.

CHAPTER 2
dna profiling

The human body grows, develops, and works according to a set of instructions inside its cells. The instructions are stored in a substance called DNA (deoxyribonucleic acid). Apart from identical twins, everyone's DNA is different. This gives scientists a way to identify someone from blood or other body matter left at the scene of a crime.

Genetic fingerprints When blood, other body fluid, or tissue is found at a crime scene, it is used to produce a DNA profile. This is also known as a genetic fingerprint, because it is unique

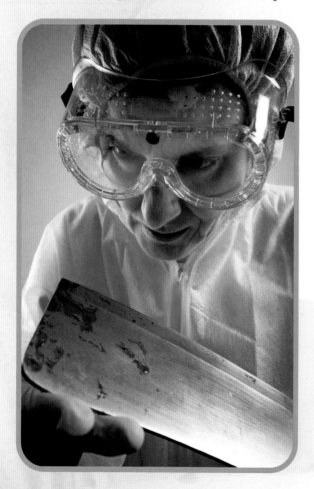

HOW IT WORKS

There are several ways to produce a DNA profile. One way produces a profile called an autoradiograph. This looks like a stack of short lines. First, the DNA is cut into short fragments by enzymes. The fragments are placed at one end of a sheet of gel. Electricity draws the fragments through the gel. Short fragments travel faster than long fragments, so they spread out through the gel. The fragments are then absorbed onto a sheet of paper, which is exposed to radiation. The fragments become radioactive. A sheet of photographic film is laid on top of the paper and the DNA produces dark lines on the film. The result can be compared with another autoradiograph to find out if there is a match.

A bloodstain at a crime scene contains enough information to identify the person it belongs to.

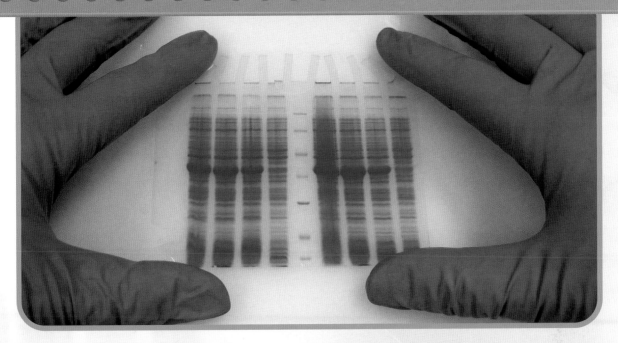

An autoradiograph, also known as a genetic fingerprint, is made up of stacks of bands. The pattern of bands is different for each person.

to each person in the same way as a fingerprint. If a crime scene DNA profile matches a suspect's DNA profile, it proves that the suspect was present at the crime scene. DNA profiling was invented by Alec Jeffreys at Leicester University in England in 1984.

DNA databases In some countries, the DNA profiles of criminals are stored in a database. DNA collected later from crime scenes is compared to profiles in the database to see if there is a match. Ideally, investigators look for a perfect match, but a partial match is also possible. A partial match means that the crime scene DNA may have come from a close relative of the person

FOR AND AGAINST

For

- A DNA database helps the police to solve crimes quickly, perhaps before a criminal can strike again.

- It finds criminals who would not be found by any other means.

- It can prove someone's innocence.

Against

- The most effective DNA database would include everyone's DNA, but many innocent people do not want their DNA stored.

- Many people do not trust governments to store DNA information securely.

- A national DNA database is very costly to set up and operate.

CASE STUDY

In the 1980s, the police in Leicestershire, England, were trying to solve two similar murders. They asked Professor Alec Jeffreys to use his DNA profiling technique to help them. Using evidence from the crimes, Jeffreys' profiles proved that the murders were committed by the same person, but not by the police's prime suspect. Five thousand men in the area of the murders were tested, but none of them was the killer. Later, the police learned that one man, Colin Pitchfork, had asked a friend to give a sample in his place. When he was tested, his DNA profile matched the killer's. He was the first person in the world to be convicted of murder as a result of DNA profiling.

whose DNA is in the database. The FBI's CODIS (Combined DNA Index System) contains more than 6.5 million DNA profiles. In 2008, it was used in more than 80,000 crime investigations.

Alec Jeffreys, the inventor of DNA profiling, looks at a profile. In 1987, his invention was used to identify and convict the murderer Colin Pitchfork. Since then, DNA profiling has helped to solve many crimes.

Contamination It is vital to stop unwanted DNA getting into a crime scene. Before forensic scientists enter a crime scene, they dress to stop any of their hair, skin cells, sweat, or clothing fibers from falling onto anything. They wear surgical gloves, a face mask, and a suit that covers their whole body, including their hair.

Smaller samples The first DNA profiling methods needed large samples—a few drops of blood. Now, forensic scientists can create a profile from as little as a few cells. They do it by copying this tiny amount of DNA thousands of times until there is enough to test.

Mixed-up DNA About 10 percent of the DNA samples collected from crime scenes can't be analyzed because they contain the DNA of two or more people mixed together. The British Forensic Science Service has developed new computer software that can unscramble the DNA and produce separate profiles. The software is called DNAboost, and it will enable scientists to reinvestigate past unsolved crimes.

DNA

In 1953 at Cambridge University in England, scientists James Watson and Francis Crick discovered that DNA looks like a spiral-shaped ladder. This coiled shape is called a double helix. Two strands of molecules called sugar-phosphate backbones make up the sides of the ladder. Chemical units called base pairs connect the two strands like the rungs of a ladder. There are four kinds of bases, and the order in which they occur is different in each person.

DNA curls around itself in a shape that is called a double helix.

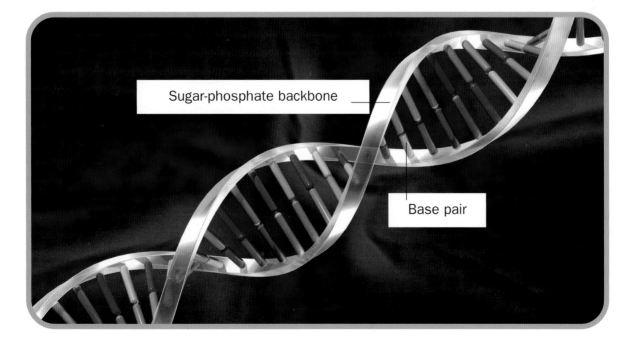

Sugar-phosphate backbone

Base pair

Moments after his release from prison in 2008, Steven Barnes is reunited with his mother and sister. New DNA tests proved his innocence.

Guilty or innocent DNA is equally useful for proving that someone did not commit a crime. There are many cases where a suspect is identified, but DNA proves that someone else committed the crime. In the United States, more than 240 prisoners have been freed as a result of DNA testing. They were people who had been convicted of crimes in the years before DNA profiling was available. When evidence from their cases was reexamined using the latest DNA techniques, they were proved innocent.

CASE STUDY

In 1989, at the age of 23, Steven Barnes was convicted of murder and imprisoned for 25 years to life. Nearly 20 years later, DNA analysis of the victim's clothing proved that Barnes did not commit the crime. He was released in 2008, a completely innocent man. DNA tests had been carried out in 1993, but the techniques available then were not sensitive enough to produce a genetic profile of the attacker. The case was reopened in 2007, and more advanced tests were able to show that the attacker's DNA did not belong to Steven Barnes.

Ivory smuggling Animal DNA can be used to solve crimes, too. Experts think that thousands of elephants are killed in Africa every year for the ivory in their tusks. Customs officers and police departments often discover illegal shipments of tusks in far-flung parts of the world. Until recently, there was no way to find out where in Africa the elephant tusks had come from.

Researchers in the United States have found a way to use elephant DNA to trace the origin of illegal tusks. It's difficult and dangerous to take blood samples from wild elephants. Instead, the scientists collected dung from herds of elephants all over Africa and used it to create DNA profiles for the animals in each area. They can now compare the DNA profiles of tusks seized anywhere in the world with their elephant DNA map of Africa to find out where the elephants were killed. This information is then sent to law

WHAT'S NEXT?

Researchers at the University of Arizona have developed a way of predicting what a person looks like by analyzing their DNA, something that has never been done before. They noted the hair, skin, and eye color of about 1,000 people and compared them to the parts of the DNA that form these characteristics. In the future, this may enable forensic scientists to produce rough descriptions of people from samples of their DNA.

enforcement officers in the areas where poachers are killing elephants, so that the herds can be better protected.

DNA profiling is helping to combat the serious problem of elephant poaching in Africa and the illegal trade in elephant tusks.

CHAPTER 3
fire and explosion

Fires and explosions are used by criminals and terrorists to kill people, destroy property, make fraudulent insurance claims, or destroy evidence of other crimes. The specialists who investigate these events are experts in making sense of the jumble of blackened debris left after a fire or explosion.

Finding clues Investigators can tell where a fire started and how it spread just by looking at the pattern of burning and blackening on floors, walls, ceilings, and furniture. Explosion experts can search through tons of debris and find tiny parts of a bomb that survived an explosion. Back in the lab, science and technology yield even more information.

A fire inspector examines the scene of a fire to determine how the fire started.

ARSON

Accidental fires usually start in one place, called the fire's point of origin. If investigators find two or more points of origin, they suspect the fire may have been deliberately started. This type of crime is known as arson. If arson is suspected, investigators will look more closely at the cause of the fire. They pay special attention to any evidence suggesting that it may not have been accidental.

Gas or another flammable liquid is often used to start a fire. A substance used for this purpose is called an accelerant. Pieces of soft materials such as wood, carpet, or furnishings that might have absorbed vapors from an accelerant are sealed in airtight containers and taken to a lab. There, a vacuum pump sucks out the vapors and sends them to a piece of equipment called a gas chromatograph. This tells investigators which accelerant was used.

Investigators may then be able to find traces of the same substance on a suspect's body or clothes, or find a similar substance in a suspect's home. They may be able to show that a suspect bought the same substance just before the crime was committed.

A gas chromatograph can identify tiny traces of substances found at the scene of a crime.

HOW IT WORKS

An unknown substance is carried into a gas chromatograph by a stream of gas called the carrier gas. Helium or nitrogen is normally used because they will not alter the unknown substance. The substance works its way through a long, thin pipe packed with particles coated with liquid. The pipe, called the column, may be up to 33 feet (10 m) long, but less than 0.08 inch (2 mm) wide. Small, light molecules travel through the column faster than big, heavy molecules. The smallest molecules come out of the end of the column first, and the bigger ones follow. As each type of molecule reaches the end of the column, a detector identifies it. The results appear on a computer screen. If the detector is a mass spectrometer (see page 10), the machine is called a GC-MS machine.

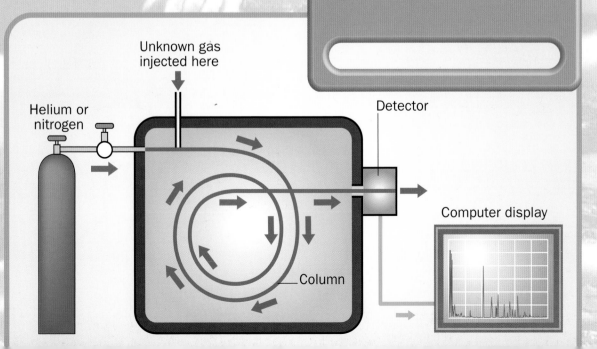

Unknown gas injected here

Helium or nitrogen

Detector

Computer display

Column

Explosive detectors Explosive detection equipment can identify explosives in a few seconds on the spot, without having to send samples to a lab for analysis. These detectors are commonly used at places like airports.

Investigators comb the scene of an explosion, searching for clues of the cause.

A small piece of paper or cloth called a swatch is wiped over a suspect's luggage and then placed in the instrument. Particles picked up by the

HOW IT WORKS

Debris flies out in all directions from an explosion at up to 6,800 mph (11,000 kph), or about nine times the speed of sound. Experienced explosion investigators can often tell what caused an explosion by the type of damage at the scene. Gas explosions produce a pushing effect on everything around them. High explosives detonate faster than gas and have a shattering effect on everything nearby.

Good vibrations Teams of researchers in Tennessee and Denmark have developed a new way to detect explosives. They use tiny, inexpensive sensors called micromechanical devices. When molecules of explosives floating in the air settle on the sensor, they produce tiny mechanical movements. These movements produce electronic signals, which can be measured and analyzed. Different molecules produce different signals that let the device determine what the molecules are and identify the type of explosive.

swatch are charged with electricity and sent flying through a short tube. The particles are slowed down by gas inside the tube. Big particles slow down more than small particles. The time it takes the different-sized particles to arrive at the end of the tube tells the detector what they are and identifies any explosives that are present. This type of detector is called an ion mobility spectrometer (IMS).

IMS detectors are used to find illegal drugs, too. Compared to a GC-MS machine, an IMS detector is smaller, lighter, simpler, and works faster. This makes it ideal for security or customs officers to use it without scientific training.

WHAT'S NEXT?

In the future, it may be possible to detect explosives from a distance just by using light. Researchers at the University of Florida have succeeded in detecting explosives by firing a laser at a surface with particles of explosives on it. The explosives change the laser beam's reflection in ways that a computer can recognize. Because this method of detecting explosives is quick and can be done from a distance, it could help save many lives.

CHAPTER 4
trace evidence

The smallest pieces of evidence are called trace evidence. They include hair, fibers, paint chips, tiny fragments of glass, and small amounts of unknown fluids and particles. Although small, they can sometimes lead investigators to a criminal. Trace evidence is especially useful in investigations where no DNA or fingerprints are found at the crime scene.

Hair Strands of hair found at a crime scene or in a suspect's home or car can be useful to crime investigators in several ways.

Hair is covered with scales. The scales on human hair and animal hair look different. Forensic scientists can tell whether hair is human by looking at it through a microscope. They use a light microscope for magnifications up to about 1,000 times. If more magnification is needed, they can use a scanning electron microscope (SEM). An SEM can magnify traces of evidence up to 100,000 times or more.

Strands of hair and fibers collected in different places can be compared by looking at them through a comparison microscope to see if they match. This special microscope shows both samples at the same time, side by side. A comparison microscope is also used by firearms experts to compare two bullets to see if they were fired by the same gun.

Finding poison Hair can also prove that someone was poisoned. As hair grows, it absorbs substances from inside the body. If someone was poisoned slowly over several weeks, chemical analysis of his or her hair

A comparison microscope shows a magnified image of two objects, such as bullets (shown here), hairs, or fibers, at the same time.

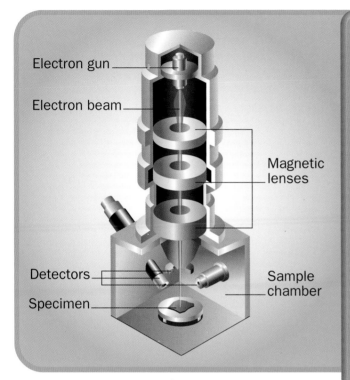

Electron gun

Electron beam

Magnetic lenses

Detectors

Specimen

Sample chamber

A scanning electron microscope (SEM) produces highly magnified images of small pieces of trace evidence.

HOW IT WORKS

A scanning electron microscope uses a beam of electrons instead of light to form images. The electrons are fired down from the top of the microscope. Magnetic lenses focus the beam on a specimen at the bottom. The beam knocks electrons out of the specimen's surface. These are collected by a detector and form a bright spot on a screen. The electron beam is scanned back and forth across the specimen, building up a picture on the screen from lines of bright spots, like a television picture.

HAIR FACTS

Human hair grows about 0.1 inch (2.5 mm) a week. Facial hair grows faster, and body hair slower. A healthy human head has about 100,000 hairs. Blondes have more hair than brunettes. Redheads have the least. About 100 hairs fall out every day, so the chance of a criminal dropping one or two hairs at the scene of a crime is quite high.

will reveal the poison. A hair that has the root attached to it can be used to find the owner's blood type and DNA profile. Scientists can also tell from the root whether the hair fell out or was pulled out.

Fibers Different types of man-made fibers can be hard to identify because they look alike. However, forensic scientists can tell exactly what they are by using a machine called an infrared spectroscope. The infrared part of light is the invisible part just beyond the red end of the spectrum. Infrared light is shined on the fibers and they absorb,

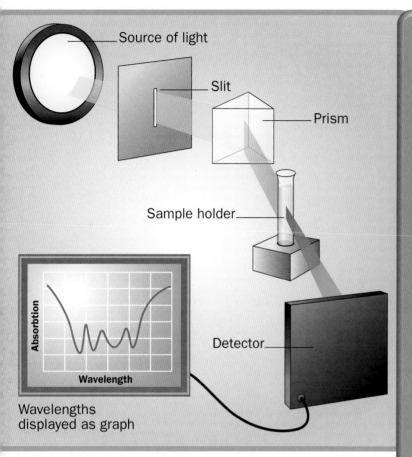

Source of light

Slit

Prism

Sample holder

Absorbtion

Wavelength

Detector

Wavelengths
displayed as graph

A spectroscope is used to measure how light is reflected or absorbed by an unknown substance, allowing scientists to identify that substance.

HOW IT WORKS

A spectroscope is an instrument for analyzing light. It is also called a spectrometer. Ultraviolet, infrared, or visible light enters the instrument and is spread out into the different wavelengths it contains. This is done by a prism or a device called a diffraction grating. This is a glass or polished metal surface with many parallel grooves. Each wavelength travels through an unknown sample or reflects off it. A detector measures the way the sample changes the light. The intensities of the different wavelengths are displayed on a screen. Each substance absorbs or reflects the light in a unique way, enabling a scientist to identify a substance.

or soak up, some of the light. Different types of fibers absorb different parts of the light. The spectroscope shows which part of the light the fibers have absorbed, and this identifies the substance they are made of.

Tiny paint chips are analyzed in the same way. It may be possible to match paint chips found at the scene of a crime to a suspect's car. Tiny samples of drugs can be identified like this, too.

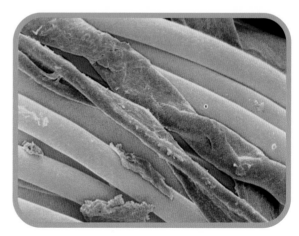

Color added to a scanning electron microscope image shows different types of fibers more clearly.

The advantage of infrared spectroscopy over some other methods is that it does not destroy or alter the sample it in any way.

Body fluids Blood, saliva, and other body fluids can be difficult to see, especially if they are on colored materials or have been cleaned up. Forensic scientists search for them by using special flashlights. These bright lights can have filters put on that produce colored light. Violet or blue light is good for finding body fluids.

Forensic scientists searching for evidence sometimes use special flashlights that make body fluids show up more clearly.

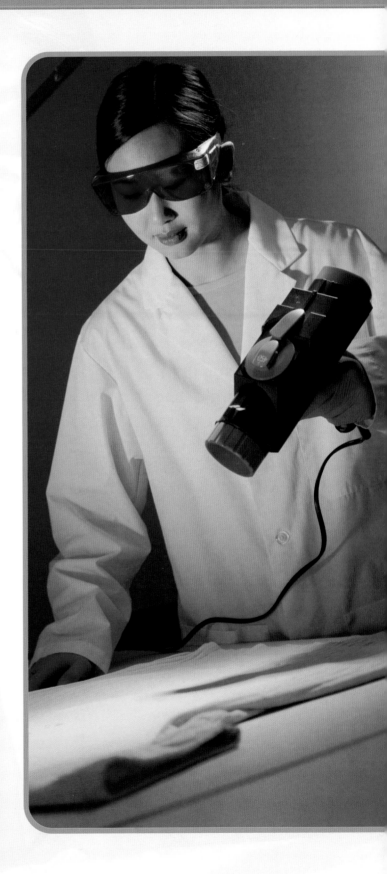

BLOOD

An adult human has 4 to 6 quarts (4 to 6 L) of blood. Everyone's blood looks the same, but there are different types of blood. There are four main blood types, called A, B, O, and AB. They were discovered in the early 1900s by Karl Landsteiner at the University of Vienna, Austria. Landsteiner's work made it possible for doctors to tranfuse blood safely from one person to another. Until then, mixing blood types could make the blood cells stick together, which could be fatal.

Thieves often break windows to get into a building. Samples of broken glass collected from a crime scene can provide evidence linking a person to a crime.

changes at a known rate. When the glass and the oil have the same refractive index, the glass disappears. It cannot be seen because it bends light in exactly the same way as the surrounding oil. Another test involves examining the surface of the glass under a microscope to check its shape and look for telltale marks that show how it was manufactured.

Finally, scientists find out the chemical makeup of the glass. They fire a laser at it to heat a tiny spot so much that it vaporizes (changes to gas). This is called laser ablation. The gas is then

Glass If glass is broken during a crime, tiny fragments of the glass may land on the hair and clothing of anyone within 6 to 9 feet (2 to 3 m). Some of these fragments may be no bigger than a grain of sand. Investigators who find this glass on a suspect want to prove where it came from, because it could show that a suspect was at the crime scene when the crime happened.

There are a number of tests that scientists can perform on glass to help them identify where it came from. They can measure how much it bends light, called its refractive index. They do this by heating up the glass in a dish of oil. As the oil warms up, its refractive index

WHAT'S NEXT?

In the future, trace evidence could be added deliberately to things that might be handled by a criminal. Bullets may be dusted with microscopic particles called nanotags. The tags will rub off onto the hands and clothes of anyone who handles the bullets and can be found by forensic scientists. In this way, they can prove that the person handled the ammunition.

Fragments of glass can be analyzed by a mass spectrometer to find their chemical makeup.

analyzed by a mass spectrometer, which shows exactly what it is made of. After this battery of tests, forensic scientists can say whether or not fragments of glass on a suspect's hair and clothes match glass from the crime scene.

NANOTAGS

Nanotags are microscopic particles made in a lab from plant pollen. In nature, pollen carries the male parts of a flower to the female parts. Pollen grains are very sticky. They stick to any surface they touch, however shiny and smooth it is. Scientists coat the pollen grains with a cocktail of chemicals including titanium oxide, zirconia, and silica. The precise quantities of all the chemicals in the mixture can be altered in a very accurate way from one batch of bullets to another, so each batch has a unique chemical label to identify it.

These are nanotags, microscopic pollen grains coated with chemicals. They could help to catch criminals who use guns.

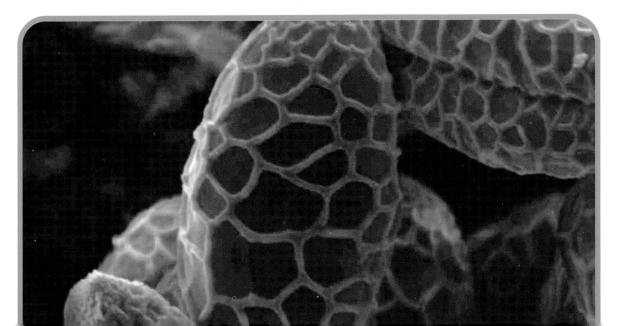

CHAPTER 5
investigating death

When someone dies in mysterious circumstances or as a result of a crime, it is vital to know what caused the person's death. An examination of the body called an autopsy takes place. The word autopsy comes from Greek words meaning "I see for myself," because a forensic scientist opens up the body and looks inside.

Autopsy An autopsy begins with a careful examination of the victim's skin. Marks and injuries are examined closely and photographed. Hair samples, fingernail scrapings, blood, and other samples are taken from the body at this stage.

Next, the body is opened by using a Y-shaped cut extending from the shoulders all the way down the front of the body. The organs are taken out, weighed, and examined. The brain is removed, too. The stomach contents and slices of the organs are taken for further examination. Anything that looks abnormal is noted.

From start to finish, an autopsy takes anywhere from an hour for a simple case to six hours for a complicated one. The basic technology used hasn't changed in centuries—a surgical knife and a set of scales to weigh the organs. However, the techniques used for detecting chemicals in the body and damage to the organs has improved.

A forensic scientist prepares to open a body and perform an autopsy.

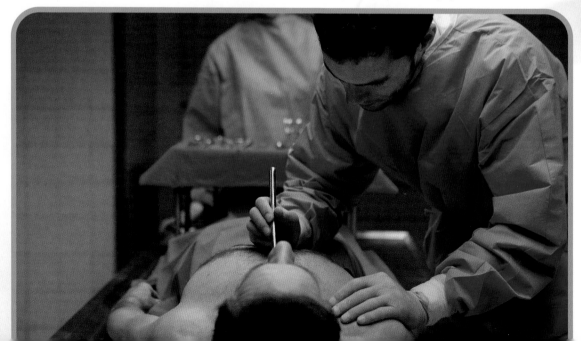

Virtual autopsy Scientists are experimenting in discovering the causes of death without cutting a body open. They are doing this by scanning bodies with a CT scanner and an MRI scanner. A CT scanner shows the bony skeleton clearly, while the MRI scanner shows the soft tissue. By combining the scans, it is possible to produce a 3D see-through image of the body that a forensic scientist can examine. This type of autopsy is called a virtual autopsy. It is also possible for forensic scientists to perform this type of autopsy over the Internet. In the future, most autopsies could be carried out in this way.

HOW IT WORKS

A magnetic resonance imaging (MRI) scanner uses a powerful magnet to make the hydrogen atoms in a patient's body line up in the same direction. Then a pulse of radio waves pushes these atoms in a different direction. When the pulse is turned off, the atoms swing back and give out a small burst of energy. This is transformed into images of slices through the body.

A doctor examines a CT scan of the brain. Forensic scientists sometimes use CT scans like this to help them discover the cause of death.

HOW IT WORKS

A computed tomography (CT) scanner is a machine with a hole in the middle where a patient lies. An X-ray machine in the ring around the hole takes a series of X-ray images as it rotates around the patient. Beams of X-rays that pass through dense tissue such as bone are weakened more than beams that pass through soft tissue. A computer combines all the images to produce pictures of slices through parts of the patient's body.

A forensic scientist uses ground penetrating radar to search for buried evidence.

Finding bodies Investigators may sometimes suspect that someone has been killed, but they can't find a body. If they suspect that the body might have been buried, they can use radar to look for it. Radar finds things by sending out radio waves and looking for reflections that bounce back from something. Crime investigators use a special type of radar designed to look down into the ground, called ground penetrating radar. As the radar is moved along the ground, it sends radio waves downward. These are reflected by underground layers of soil, and the layers appear on a screen. A buried body disturbs the natural

layers, and this shows up clearly on the machine's screen.

Thermal cameras (cameras that detect heat) can also be used to search for buried bodies. Disturbed soil has a cooler temperature from that of undisturbed soil. A search for a hidden grave is made by scanning the ground with a thermal camera from the air. The aerial search turns up points of interest on the ground that search teams can then look at more closely.

Making faces Nearly all bodies have already been identified by the time an autopsy is performed, but sometimes a body cannot be identified. It may have been too badly damaged, too badly decomposed, or it may have been

HOW IT WORKS

Traditional facial reconstruction involves sticking pegs to a plaster copy of a skull at key points called landmarks. The pegs are the same length as the depth of muscle and skin at the landmarks. Then muscles and skin made of clay are added so that the pegs are just covered. The end result is usually close enough to the person's appearance to enable friends or relatives to recognize the face.

undiscovered for so long that only a skeleton remains. One way to identify a body is to use the skull to reconstruct what the person looked like in life. The traditional way to do this is to sculpt the face in clay. A forensic artist or a forensic anthropologist does this work. Now there are facial reconstruction programs that will do the same thing on a computer screen. The skull is scanned into a computer, which then adds the muscles and skin. Skin color, eye color, hair color, and hairstyle can be changed with a click of a mouse.

Forensic facial reconstruction is the process of recreating the face of an unidentified person from their remains. Today, computer programs are sometimes used to do this.

CASE STUDY

In 1970, a woman's body was found in Ohio, but she could not be identified. In 2007, after the case was reopened, a clay head was made from the skull to reconstruct the victim's face. When photographs of the clay head were published, Phyllis Nichols thought it looked like her missing niece from Wisconsin. In 2009, a comparison of DNA samples from the body and the family confirmed the person's identity as Jeanne Marie Melville from Green Bay, Wisconsin.

CHAPTER 6

fakes and forgeries

Fakers and forgers try their best to produce documents and works of art that aren't what they seem. Forensic scientists have developed a variety of techniques and technology for detecting their criminal activity. Forged documents can often be detected by something as simple as colored light.

The light test The simplest forgeries to detect are documents that have been altered by adding extra words or numbers. A forger might try to change a check for $10 into one for $10,000. The ink used to make the change is almost certainly different from the original ink on the check. The two inks might look the same in ordinary daylight, but their different chemical make-up becomes clear under special lighting.

A forensic document examiner tests a suspicious document by shining different colors of light on it inside a light-proof box. A video camera sends a picture of the document to a screen. If the document has been altered, the changes show up clearly, because the two inks react differently to the colored light. Dollar bills and secure documents such as passports often have security markers that are invisible in daylight, but glow under special lighting.

Suspicious documents are examined under colored light to see if they are genuine or forged. The light reveals reflective patterns on a genuine passport.

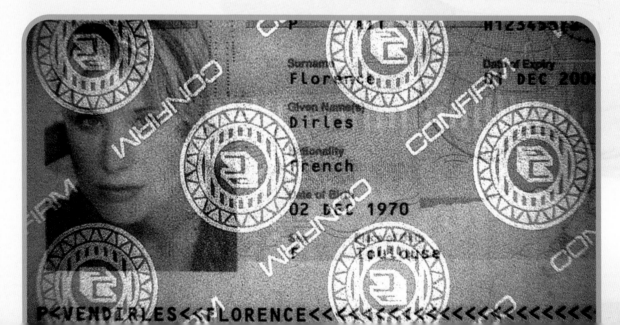

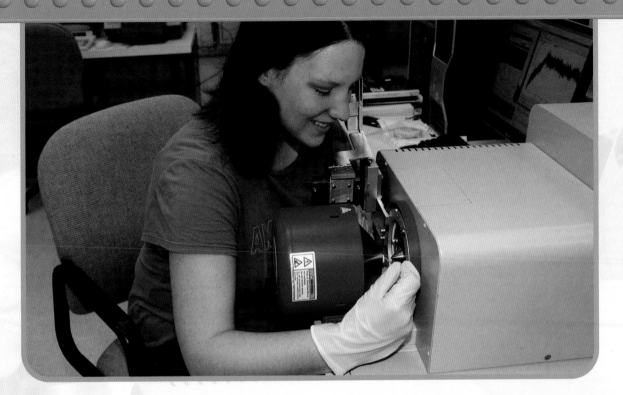

Ink library Scientists at Iowa State University are creating a library of inks that will let document specialists spot fraudulent documents more easily. Secure documents such as dollar bills, checks, and some official certificates are printed with particular inks. Each ink has a unique chemical composition that can't be faked. The scientists are recording the chemical signatures of these inks. Forensic scientists will be able to check the ink on a suspicious document against the ink library to make sure it is genuine. Previously, this could only be done by cutting off a small piece of the document to analyze the ink on it, but the new method does not damage the document at all. It is called DART mass spectrometry. DART stands for Direct Analysis in Real Time.

A researcher prepares to analyze an ink sample using the newly developed DART mass spectrometry equipment.

HOW IT WORKS

In DART mass spectrometry, a stream of warm gas is aimed at a document. It makes molecules of ink evaporate from the paper. A mass spectrometer analyzes these molecules. The spectrometer produces a wiggly line, called a mass spectrum, on a screen or paper that represents the chemical makeup of the ink. Identical inks produce identical spectra.

Art forgery A painting by a famous artist who died long ago may be very valuable. Art forgers try to fake old paintings and sell the fakes for huge amounts of money. Sometimes, they take a worthless old canvas with a painting already on it and make a new painting on top. Forensic scientists check a painting by X-raying it. The X-ray shows the layers of paint hidden under the surface. Art experts can often tell from this whether the painting is genuine or not.

The chemistry of the paint used to make a painting can reveal whether it is genuine or fake.

Testing paint The chemicals in paint itself can give away a fake. The white paint used by artists in past centuries was made from lead with other elements in different amounts depending on where and when the paint was made. In the early 1900s, the poisonous lead in white paint was replaced by titanium. These telltale chemical differences enable forensic scientists to check whether a painting is genuine.

How old? Forgers often try to make a work of art look older than it really is. However, scientists can measure the

real age of works of art, especially those made of plant material such as wood and canvas. While a plant is alive, it takes in carbon dioxide from the air. Some of the carbon becomes part of the plant. There are different types of carbon, called isotopes. One is called carbon-14. When a plant dies, it stops taking in carbon. The carbon-14 inside it breaks down at a steady rate. Measuring how much of the carbon-14 has disappeared shows how long ago the plant died. This technique is called carbon dating.

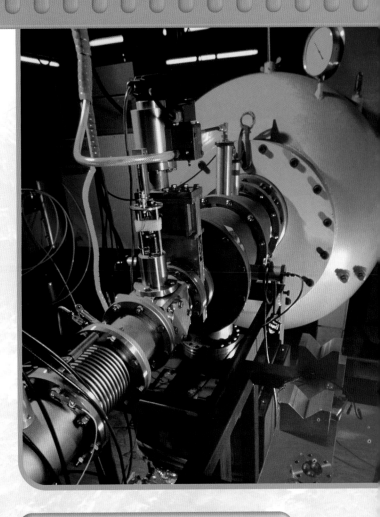

Carbon dating needs complex lab equipment to count the numbers of carbon atoms present in a sample.

FOR AND AGAINST

For
- Carbon dating can give the age of a very old work of art.
- It works for anything made from wood or other once-living material.

Against
- A small part of the artwork must be cut out and destroyed to do the test.
- It is not a reliable method for dating works of art made of materials less than about 250 years old.

DATING

Carbon dating can find the age of once-living materials that are up to about 60,000 years old. Samples older than this have too little carbon-14 left to measure. Since the beginning of the Industrial Revolution, human activities have poured extra carbon into the atmosphere. This makes carbon dating unreliable for samples from the 18th century to the present day.

Rare Ming jar or modern fake? A mass spectrometer can provide the answer.

Antique fraud Scientists at the University of Western Australia have found a way to tell the difference between valuable ancient porcelain ceramic works of art, such as antique vases, and clever modern fakes. They use a laser to vaporize a tiny spot of unglazed porcelain at the base of the item. The laser makes a pit that is not even as deep as a strand of hair. The vaporized porcelain is sucked into a mass spectrometer, which produces a detailed chemical breakdown of the porcelain. The levels of elements in the porcelain are then compared to samples from many places and dates to find out where and when it was made.

The technique is sensitive enough to enable experts to find out where the clay used to make the porcelain was dug out of the ground. It can also be used to trace where the porcelain was fired and the time period when it was manufactured. If a vase that is supposed to be a valuable 15th century Chinese work of art is found to be made from clay that was not used in 15th century China, then the vase is a fake.

WHAT'S NEXT?

In the future, the image, X-ray, and chemical fingerprint of every work of art could be recorded in a database. This would make it impossible to sell a stolen work of art or pass off a fake as the real thing. Having an official record of these details would make it easy to check out a work of art in the same way as police officers can check out a car and within seconds know its history, insurance status, and ownership.

A gas chromatograph can tell the difference between fake fuel and the real thing.

Fake fuel Ordinary things, not just valuable works of art, are faked if criminals think they can make money off of them. Fake fuel is a big earner in some countries. Criminals buy cheap fuel and disguise it as a different fuel that is more expensive or heavily taxed, such as diesel. When they sell the fake fuel at the full price, they make a big profit. In the past, fuels were labeled by adding telltale colors or chemicals, but criminals quickly learned how to fake these markers.

Now, Japanese scientists have developed a new way to identify a fuel by measuring how much sulfur it contains. Sulfur is a chemical element found in the oil that fuel is made from. Different fuels contain different amounts of sulfur. The amount of sulfur is measured by using a gas chromatograph (see page 21). No matter what a fuel appears to be, the sulfur test shows what it really is. The scientists have found that they can use this same method to identify fuel used to start a fire in cases of arson.

CHAPTER 7
cyber forensics

Digital equipment, including computers and cell phones, is seized from suspects in almost every criminal investigation. Specialists in forensic digital analysis examine the equipment and retrieve useful information from it. Cyber forensics, or digital forensics, is becoming increasingly important in crime fighting.

Getting information Investigators can retrieve a lot of information from digital devices such as computer discs, cell phones, MP3 or MP4 players, personal digital assistants (PDAs), or digital cameras. In addition to text and images, there is also hidden information, recorded automatically by the device. It may show when the text or images were recorded, when they were updated, and even sometimes who recorded the information.

CASE STUDY

When the British serial killer Dr. Harold Shipman was arrested in 1998, investigators examined patient records on his computer. When he killed a patient, he altered the patient's medical record to match the story he told relatives about the death. He did not realize that the computer recorded details of these alterations, which investigators were able to retrieve.

Phone data Most cell phones contain a Subscriber Identity Module (SIM) card. It stores information about the phone and its user, a directory of phone numbers saved by the user, and text messages. It may even hold retrievable information about where it was used in the past. A digital forensics specialist

Computer hard drives can yield a great deal of information, much of it hidden from the user.

can extract this information from the card. Deleted text messages can usually be retrieved, too. The phone, or just its SIM card, is plugged into a reader, which displays the card's contents on a computer screen. Records of calls and texts can lead the police to new suspects or witnesses, who may hold the key to solving the crime.

The game's up One of the latest developments in cyber forensics is a kit that lets scientists search the hard drive of a video game console for data. Criminals sometimes use video game console hard drives for storing illegal material in the hope that investigators will not search there.

Serial killer Dennis Rader is escorted to prison to begin his life sentence.

conclusion

With every year that passes, forensic science and technology advance further and are used more effectively to provide evidence to convict criminals. It is difficult to predict the future with any accuracy, but one thing is certain. Future forensic science and technology will be even more effective in bringing criminals to justice.

Tiny scraps Forensic scientists have developed methods and technology for analyzing smaller and smaller scraps of evidence, and this trend will continue. It is already possible to collect and analyze evidence so small that it can't be seen with the naked eye. In the future, it will become more difficult for criminals, even the most careful and smart criminals, to be at a crime scene without leaving measurable evidence behind and taking measurable evidence away with them. However, any new tests and technologies that are developed will have to be faster and less expensive than existing methods. If they aren't, law enforcement agencies won't have enough time or money to use them.

Truth or lies? Criminals and terrorists often have information that investigators want to know about, but it can be difficult to decide if suspects are lying or withholding information when they are questioned. Lie detectors can help. Traditional lie detectors work by detecting physical changes that happen when someone lies, such as sweating or a quickening pulse. The results can be difficult to interpret. A new technique uses an MRI body scanner to detect lies by analyzing brain activity directly. In tests, it is said to be 97 percent accurate.

In the future, fingerprint scanners could be built into glass doors, identifying people as they push them open.

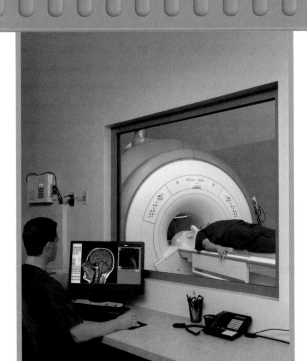

A brain scanner can tell the difference between truth and lies. Maybe one day investigators will use MRI scanners, like this one, to observe suspects' brain activity during questioning.

Predicting crimes The movie *Minority Report* shows police officers arresting people before they could commit crimes. That was fiction, but the U.S. Department of Homeland Security has been testing a real system, called Future Attribute Screening Technology (FAST), designed to predict which people are most likely to commit crimes. It works by analyzing their heart rate, temperature, breathing, and tiny muscle movements in their face. All of this can be done automatically by a scanner from a distance without their knowledge.

WHAT'S NEXT?

Today, people arriving at national borders and secure buildings have their identity checked and they may be filmed by CCTV (Closed-Circuit Television). In the future, they may be scanned for signs of criminal intentions by cameras linked to powerful computers. Technology has a habit of becoming cheaper and more widely available over time. Perhaps this technology will appear in banks and stores one day in the future.

FOR AND AGAINST

Predicting criminals and crimes:
For
• A system that can predict when someone is about to commit a crime could save the lives of many people.

Against
• If the system makes mistakes, innocent people might be put on record as possible terrorists.

• People feel that this system would be an invasion of their privacy.

glossary

accelerant a substance, such as gas, used to speed up the spread of a fire in cases of arson

arson the crime of deliberately setting fire to a building or other property

autopsy an examination of a body after death to find out why the person died

autoradiograph an image on film showing a DNA profile

carbon dating a method for measuring the age of once-living objects or material

corrosion damage on metal caused by chemical reactions; rust on iron and steel is corrosion.

CT scanner a machine that takes X-ray pictures of a patient from different angles and then combines them to produce pictures of slices through the body

cyber forensics a branch of forensic science that deals with evidence in computers and other digital devices

decomposed decayed or rotted away

DNA deoxyribonucleic acid; the substance containing the genetic code that controls the growth and functioning of organisms, including human beings

DNA database a library of DNA profiles used by law enforcement agencies to identify people who leave DNA at crime scenes

DNA profile a pattern of black bars on film or a series of numbers that represents someone's unique genetic code; also called a genetic fingerprint

electron a particle of matter with a single negative electric charge

enzymes proteins made by living cells; enzymes produce a variety of chemical reactions in living organisms.

evidence the facts and items that prove the truth of what happened in a criminal case

flammable easily set on fire

forensic relating to the use of science in legal matters, for example, in gathering and analyzing evidence for use in a court of law

fraudulent dishonest or deceitful

gas chromatograph a scientific instrument that separates a substance out into the different types of atoms and molecules it contains; a detector connected to the machine then identifies them.

ion an electrically charged atom or group of atoms

laser an instrument that produces an intense beam of light

mass spectrometer a scientific instrument that identifies unknown substances

MRI scanner magnetic resonance imaging scanner; an instrument that uses a very powerful magnet and radio waves to produce pictures of slices through the body

radar radio detection and ranging; a method developed for locating aircraft and ships by sending out radio waves and receiving reflections from the aircraft and ships

radiation waves or particles given out by something

radioactive undergoing decay (changing from one element to another) by giving out particles or waves

scanning electron microscope a microscope that uses an electron beam instead of light to produce greatly magnified images of specimens

spectroscope an instrument for breaking up light into the different wavelengths it contains so that they can be studied

wavelength the distance between one peak of a wave and the next peak; we see different wavelengths of light as different colors.

X-rays invisible electromagnetic waves, similar to light but with much shorter waves; X-rays can travel through solids, some more easily than others, and darken photographic film.

more information

Books

Cool Science: Forensic Science
by Ron Fridell, Lerner, 2007.

Current Controversies: Forensic Technology
edited by Sylvia Engdahl, Greenhaven Press, 2010.

Eyewitness Books: Forensic Science
by Chris Cooper, Dorling Kindersley, 2008.

Solve That Crime! Crime Under the Microscope: In the Forensics Lab
by Carol Ballard, Enslow Publishers, 2009.

Why Science Matters: Fighting Crime
by Ian Graham, Heinemann Library, 2009.

Web Sites

Find out more about crime scene investigation at:
http://science.howstuffworks.com/csi5.htm

Read about trace evidence at:
www.michigan.gov/msp/0,1607,7-123-1593_3800-15961--,00.html

Learn more about forensic science at:
www.explainthatstuff.com/forensicscience.html

Do some forensic science experiments at:
www.hometrainingtools.com/article.asp?ai=1227&bhcd2=1251055208

Follow a crime scene investigation at:
http://pbskids.org/dragonflytv/parentsteachers/tguide_forensics.html

Places to Visit

CSI: The Experience at MGM Grand
Las Vegas, Nevada
http://lasvegas.csiexhibit.com

National Museum of Crime and Punishment
Washington, D.C.
http://www.crimemuseum.org

Canada Science and Technology Museum
Ottawa, Ontario
http://www.sciencetech.technomuses.ca/english/index.cfm

index

Numbers in *italic* refer to illustrations.

accelerants 21
AFIS 11, *11*, 12
arson 20, 21, 39
autopsy 30–31, *30*, 32
autoradiographs 14, 15, *15*, *16*

body fluids and tissue 6, 14, 24, 25, 27, 41
  blood 6, 14, *14*, 25, 27
  saliva 27
  sweat 9
bullets 12, 13, *13*, 24, 28, 29

carbon dating 37, *37*
cartridge cases 12–13
CCTV 43
cell phones 40
chemical analyzers 7
colored light 27, *27*, 34, *34*
comparison microscope 24, *24*
computers 7, 10, 11, 17, 23, 33, 40, 41, 43
contamination 16
corrosion 13
CT scanners 31, *31*
cyber forensics 40–41

DART mass spectrometry 35, *35*
databases 11, 15, 16, 38
DESI-MS 10–11, *10*
digital equipment 40–41
DNA 14, 17, *17*, 18, 19
  animal DNA 19

DNAboost 17
DNA profiling 14–19, 25, 41
drugs 26

electrons 25
explosions 20, 22, 23
explosives detectors 22–23

facial reconstruction 32–33, *33*
fakes and forgeries 34–39
FAST 43
fibers 6, 24, 25, 26, *26*
fingerprint dusting 8, *8*
fingerprint identification 8, 9, 11, 12
fingerprint scanners 11, 42, *42*
fingerprints 6, 8–13, *8*, *9*
  latent prints 8
fires 20–21
flashlights 27, *27*
forensic artist 33
fuming 8

gas chromatograph 21, *21*, 39, *39*
GC-MS machines 21, 23
glass 6, 24, 28–29
guns 12–13, 24

hair 6, 24, 25

IMS 23
inks 34–35
Internet 11, 31
ions 10, 11

laser ablation 28
lasers 6, 7, 23, 28, 38
lie detectors 42
Locard's Exchange Principle 6

magnetism 10
mass spectrometers 10, *10*, 11, 21, 23, 29, *29*, 35, 38
mass spectrum 35
micromechanical devices 23
microscopes 6, 7, 12, 24, 28
MRI scanners 31, 42, 43, *43*
mud 6
MXRF 9

nanotags 28, 29, *29*
ninhydrin 8

paint 24, 26, 36
poison 24–25

radar 32, *32*
radiation 14
refractive index 28

SEM 24, 25, *25*
shoeprints 12, *12*
SIM cards 40–41
spectroscopes 25, 26, *26*, 27

thermal cameras 32
tire tracks 12
trace evidence 24–29

wireless technology 9

X-rays 6, 9, 31, 36, 38